Meadows and Hedgerows

Charlotte Guillain

www.raintreepublishers.co.uk

Visit our website to find out more information about Raintree books.

To order:

☎ Phone 0845 6044371

▤ Fax +44 (0) 1865 312263

▣ Email myorders@raintreepublishers.co.uk

Customers from outside the UK please telephone +44 1865 312262

Raintree is an imprint of Capstone Global Library Limited, a company incorporated in England and Wales having its registered office at 7 Pilgrim Street, London, EC4V 6LB – Registered company number: 6695582

Edited by Charlotte Guillain, Nancy Dickmann, and Catherine Veitch
Designed by Joanna Hinton-Malivoire
Picture research by Elizabeth Alexander and Ruth Blair
Original illustrations © Capstone Global Library
Original illustrations by Joanna Hinton-Malivoire (pp. 28, 29)
Production by Victoria Fitzgerald
Originated by Capstone Global Library Ltd
Printed and bound in China by Leo Paper Products

ISBN 978 0 431 17244 6
14 13 12 11 10
10 9 8 7 6 5 4 3 2 1

ISBN 978 0 431 17251 4
15 14 13 12 11
10 9 8 7 6 5 4 3 2 1

British Library Cataloguing in Publication Data
Guillain, Charlotte,
Meadows and hedgerows. -- (Nature trails)
577.4'6-dc22

Acknowledgements
We would like to thank the following for permission to reproduce photographs: Alamy pp. **4-5** (© George Kay), **12** (© Arco Images GmbH), **27** (© Pete Thomas); Corbis pp. **6** (© Craig Aurness), **17** (© Cath Mullen; Frank Lane Picture Agency), **20** (© Image Source), **24** (© Markus Botzek); iStockphoto pp. **9**, **8**, **13 left**, **14** (© Rui Saraiva), **15** (© Pauline Mills), **23** (© Andrew Howe), **25** (© Graham Yuile); Photolibrary pp. **7** (Gary Smith/Imagestate), **11** (John Curtis/Mauritius), **16** (Daniale Schneider/Photononstop), **18-19** (Raimund Linke/Mauritius), **22** (John Cancalosi/age footstock), **26** (Guenter Fischer/imagebroker.net); Shutterstock pp. **13 middle** (Graham Prentice), **13 right** (© Olga Utlyakova).

Cover photograph of wild flowers in Ambleside Meadow reproduced with permission of Corbis (© Ashley Cooper).

The publisher would like to thank Emma Shambrook for her assistance in the preparation of this book.

Every effort has been made to contact copyright holders of material reproduced in this book. Any omissions will be rectified in subsequent printings if notice is given to the publisher.

All the internet addresses (URLs) given in this book were valid at the time of going to press. However, due to the dynamic nature of the internet, some addresses may have changed or ceased to exist since publication. While the author and publisher regret any inconvenience this may cause readers, no responsibility for any such changes can be accepted by either the author or the publishers.

Contents

Any words appearing in the text in bold, **like this**, are explained in the glossary.

What are meadows and hedgerows?

Meadows and hedgerows are types of **habitat**. A habitat is a place where plants and animals live. A meadow is a type of **grassland**, made up of grasses and flowers, and without many trees.

A hedgerow is a line of trees and **shrubs** that are growing close together. Hedgerows keep fields separate and often grow next to roads and pathways. Many different plants and animals live in meadows and hedgerows.

In this book, the Signpost boxes ask you to find out more about animals and plants. Ask an adult to help you find information in books at school, in the library, or on the Internet.

Different grasslands and hedgerows

Most **grasslands** in Britain are used by people and their animals. There are wild grasslands where trees and bushes cannot grow. Meadows are grasslands that people cut down to provide **hay** for animals in the winter.

Animals may **graze** in a meadow after the grass has been cut.

hedgerow

Some hedgerows in Britain have been growing for hundreds of years.

People look after hedgerows. The most **ancient** hedges are what is left of woodland that was cut down for farming. Other hedges were planted not long ago, for example in gardens.

Changes through the year

blossom

Meadows and hedgerows change as the seasons change. If you visit meadows and hedgerows in spring, you will see **blossom** on hedgerow trees. In meadows you might see buttercups and oxeye daisies starting to flower and the grass will start to grow.

In summer, meadows are full of tall grasses and wild flowers and hedgerows are covered in green leaves. Meadows are cut for **hay** between June and August. In winter there are berries on branches of the hedgerows and nothing is growing in the meadows.

buttercup

oxeye daisy

Exploring meadows and hedgerows

Always make sure you are allowed to walk on land where there are meadows and hedgerows. Keep to paths so you do not damage the flowers and grass. Exploring these habitats is a lot of fun and you will find many plants and animals, especially in spring and summer.

STAY SAFE

- Never disturb animals or pull up plants in meadows or hedgerows.
- Never go into meadows where there are farm animals, unless the farmer says you can.
- Make sure you wash your hands after handling plants and soil.

What to take with you

- ✓ A notebook
- ✓ A pencil
- ✓ A magnifying glass
- ✓ A digital camera

Meadow plants

Many different types of plants grow in meadows. You will find lots of types of grasses, such as sweet vernal-grass, crested dog's-tail, and common bent. Caterpillars eat many of these grasses.

lady's bedstraw

cowslip

thistle

daisy

Meadows are full of flowers in summer, such as thistles and red clover. Other common flowers include buttercups, vetches, lady's bedstraw, and oxeye daisies. Orchids and cowslips are much rarer. Butterflies and bees come to the field for these flowers and help to **pollinate** them.

Meadow animals

Many animals and birds feed and shelter among meadow plants. There are many **minibeasts**, such as spiders, grasshoppers, and beetles. Woodlice and **springtails** live on the shady ground. Small mammals such as long-tailed field mice, voles, and shrews also live in meadows.

A harvest mouse feeds on seeds, fruits, and bulbs.

You may find grass snakes in a meadow.

Badgers and deer will visit meadows looking for food. Birds such as finches, swallows, skylarks, and flycatchers will also come looking for seeds and insects. Lapwings and skylarks may nest in the long grass. Kestrels and barn owls hover above meadows looking for mice and voles to eat.

Hedgerow trees

Hedgerows may be made up of different trees and **shrubs**, such as hazel, hawthorn, and rowan. Hedgerows often include trees that are smaller and grow closer together than the trees you find in woodland or parks and gardens.

hazelnut

The trees in a hedgerow provide many places for animals to rest, feed, nest, and hide.

Can you find out some more about common hedgerow trees?

- elder
- holly
- blackthorn
- blackberry

Hedgerow flowers and berries

In spring, hedgerows burst into bloom. Hawthorn, bramble, and elder are covered in white **blossom**. Yellow celandine flowers and bluebells may grow under the trees. As the weather warms up in summer, look out for cow parsley, nettles, foxgloves, and meadowsweet.

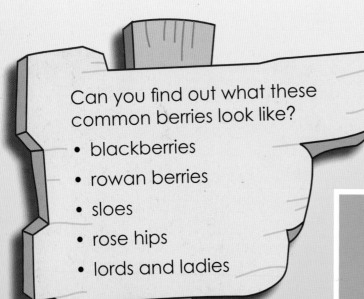

Can you find out what these common berries look like?

- blackberries
- rowan berries
- sloes
- rose hips
- lords and ladies

Brightly coloured flowers such as these dog roses attract bees that **pollinate** them.

In autumn you will find many berries growing in the hedgerow trees. Birds eat the brightly coloured fruits and spread the seeds. Never eat berries unless a trusted adult can tell you they are safe. Many berries are **poisonous** to humans.

Hedgerow minibeasts

Many small creatures live among the hedgerow leaves and in the soil at the bottom of the hedge. On summer evenings, you might spot glow worms shining. They are called "worms" but they are actually very small beetles.

On misty mornings in autumn look out for spider webs on the branches of hedgerow trees.

The life cycle of a butterfly

1 The adult female lays her eggs.

egg

5 A new adult butterfly crawls out of the pupa.

2 The **larvae** hatch from the eggs. Butterfly larvae are called caterpillars.

4 The caterpillars turn into **pupae**.

3 The caterpillars eat lots of food. They grow bigger and bigger.

Butterflies will visit different flowers and feed on their **nectar**. Look out for their caterpillars on the hedge leaves.

Can you find out about these common hedgerow minibeasts?
- cockchafer
- bee
- snail

21

Birds of the hedgerow

Many different birds feed and make their nests among the hedgerow plants. Blackbirds eat the insects in a hedge during the summer and then eat berries during winter. They often make their nests in hedges, using grass, **moss**, and mud.

Listen out for a yellowhammer as you explore a hedgerow. It sounds like it is singing "A little bit of bread and no cheese"!

Count and record

Can you count some of the different hedgerow birds you see?
Record them in a **tally chart** like this one.

Type of bird	Number spotted
blackbird	IIII
yellow hammer	I
song thrush	II
linnet	I
wood pigeon	HHH III
wren	I

Ask an adult to help you look up these birds on the RSPB website.

Hedgerow mammals

Small mammals, such as hedgehogs, weasels, and shrews live at the bottom of hedgerows. Wood mice can climb to the higher branches. Many of these animals are very shy or **nocturnal**, so they may be hard to spot.

weasel

Hedgehogs eat slugs and snails at the bottom of the hedgerow. They also eat earthworms, caterpillars, and beetles. Hedgehogs **hibernate** in piles of leaves and branches during winter. Look out for them on summer nights as they search for food.

Meadows and hedgerows in danger

Many of the wild meadows and hedgerows that used to cover Britain have gone. Many hedges that are left are **damaged** when people cut them at the wrong time of year or farm animals eat them. When these meadow and hedgerow habitats disappear, so do all the animals and plants that live there.

Many wild meadows have been used by farmers to grow crops or people have built on them.

You can help look after wild meadows and hedgerows by taking care when you visit them. Always leave things as you find them and never leave litter behind because this can hurt animals and birds.

More things to do

There are a lot more things you can do in meadows and hedgerows.

Make a meadow flower chart

Visit a local meadow in summer and make drawings of the flowers you see. When you get home, use the Internet or a flower identification book to find out what the flowers are called and label your drawings. Ask an adult to help you laminate the page, or keep it in a clear plastic folder and take it with you when you next go flower spotting.

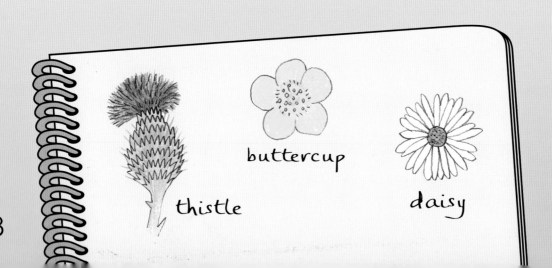

thistle

buttercup

daisy

Make a hedgerow survey

Choose a section of hedgerow near to where you live that you can visit regularly. Every month, visit the section of hedgerow and make a note of the plants, birds, and animals you can see. Take photographs or draw sketches of anything interesting you spot. Notice how the plants change in different seasons. Which plants seem to be growing well?

robin

hawthorn bush

Glossary

ancient hundreds of years old

blossom flower, usually on a fruit tree

damaged broken or hurt

grassland area of land with many grasses growing

graze eat grass. Farm animals graze.

habitat natural home of a group of plants and animals

hay grass that has been cut and dried. It is used to feed animals.

hibernate sleep during the winter when there is not much food around

larva minibeast baby that hatches from an egg. It does not look like an adult.

larvae plural of larva

minibeasts small animals, such as spiders, snails, and worms

moss small green plants that grow in damp places

nectar sweet liquid that bees collect from flowers to make honey

nocturnal active at night

pollinate take pollen from one flower to another, so new flowers can grow

poisonous may cause illness or death

pupa minibeast baby that is changing from a larva to an adult

pupae plural of pupa

shrub small, woody plant

springtail tiny minibeast

tally chart table that shows the number of something. A tally chart helps with counting.

Find out more

Books to read

Usborne Spotter's Guides: Nature (Usborne, 2008)

Help the Environment: Caring for Nature, Charlotte Guillain (Heinemann Library, 2009)

Websites and organizations

Wild Meadows
www.wildmeadows.org.uk
Wild Meadows Initiative encourages people to look after and enjoy Britain's wildflower grasslands.

The English Hedgerow Trust
www.hedgerows.co.uk
This organization tries to look after Britain's hedgerows and tells people about the plants and animals that live there.

The RSPB
www.rspb.org.uk
The Royal Society for the Protection of Birds encourages people to protect birds and the environment.

www.nationaltrust.org.uk
The National Trust may manage some interesting grassland in your area.

Index